I0442375

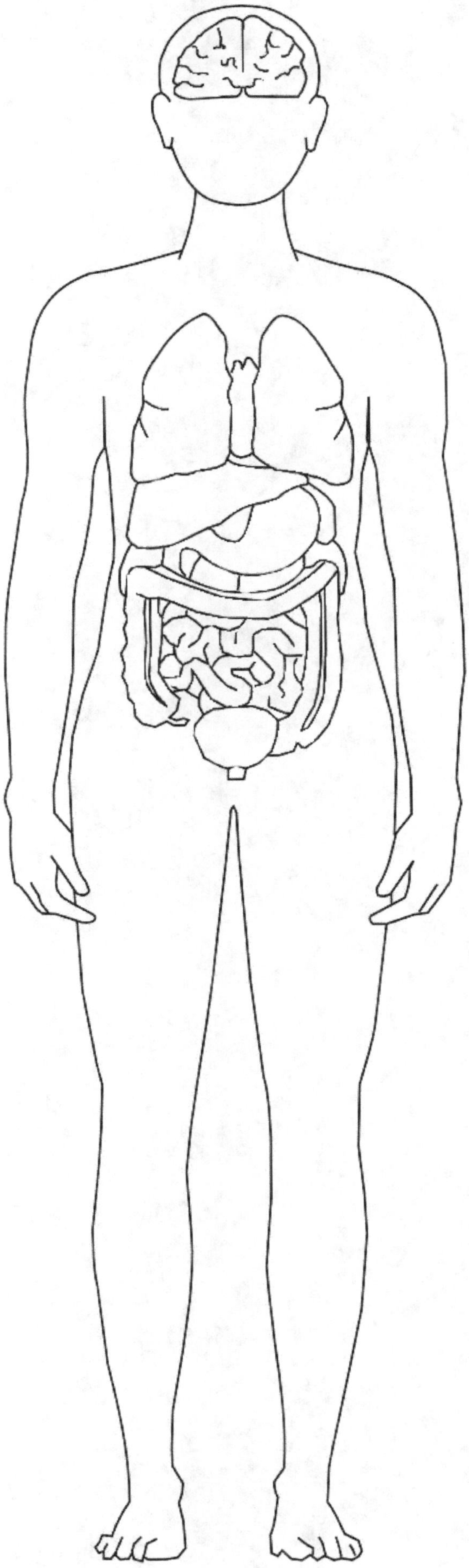

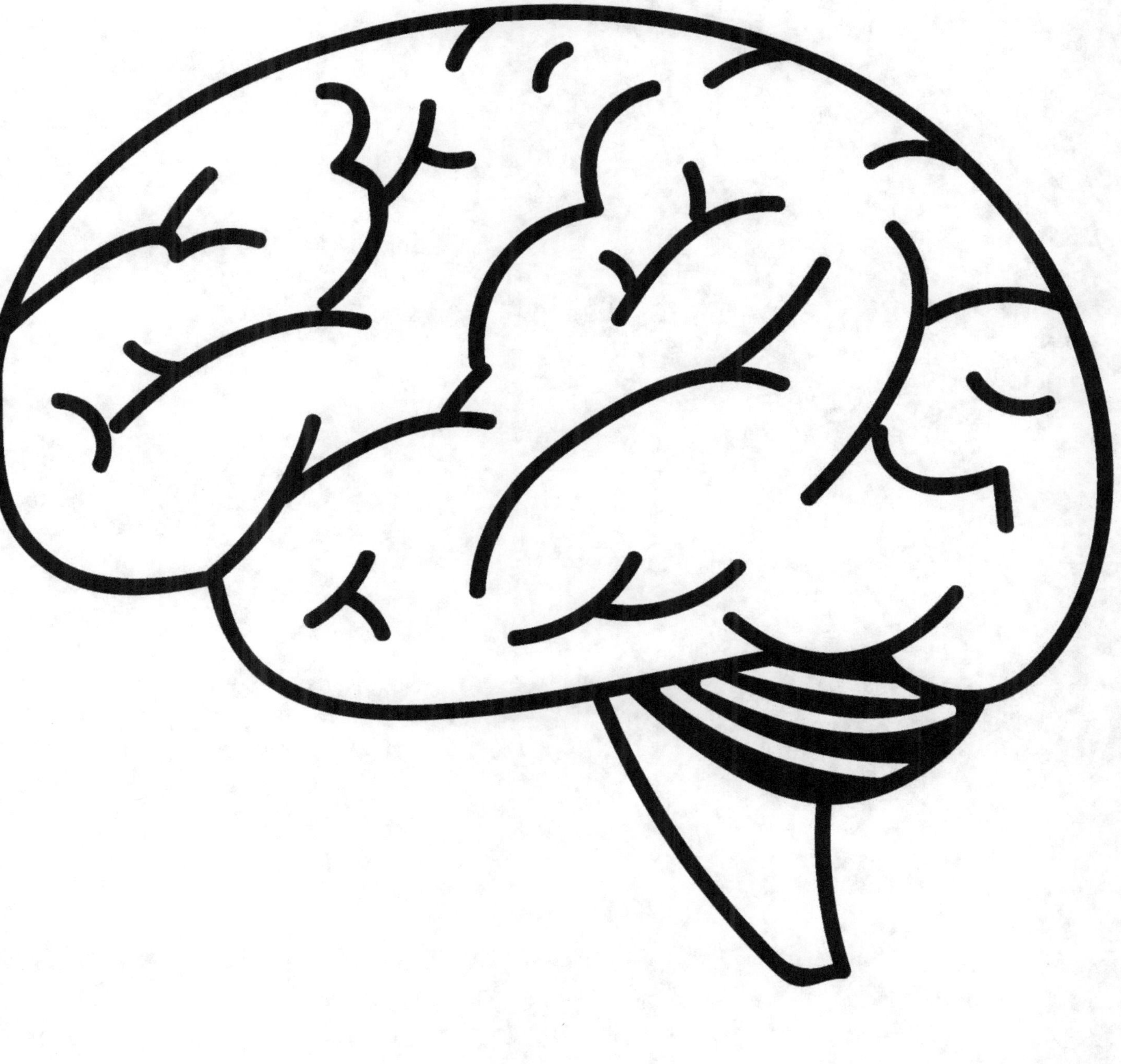

BRAIN

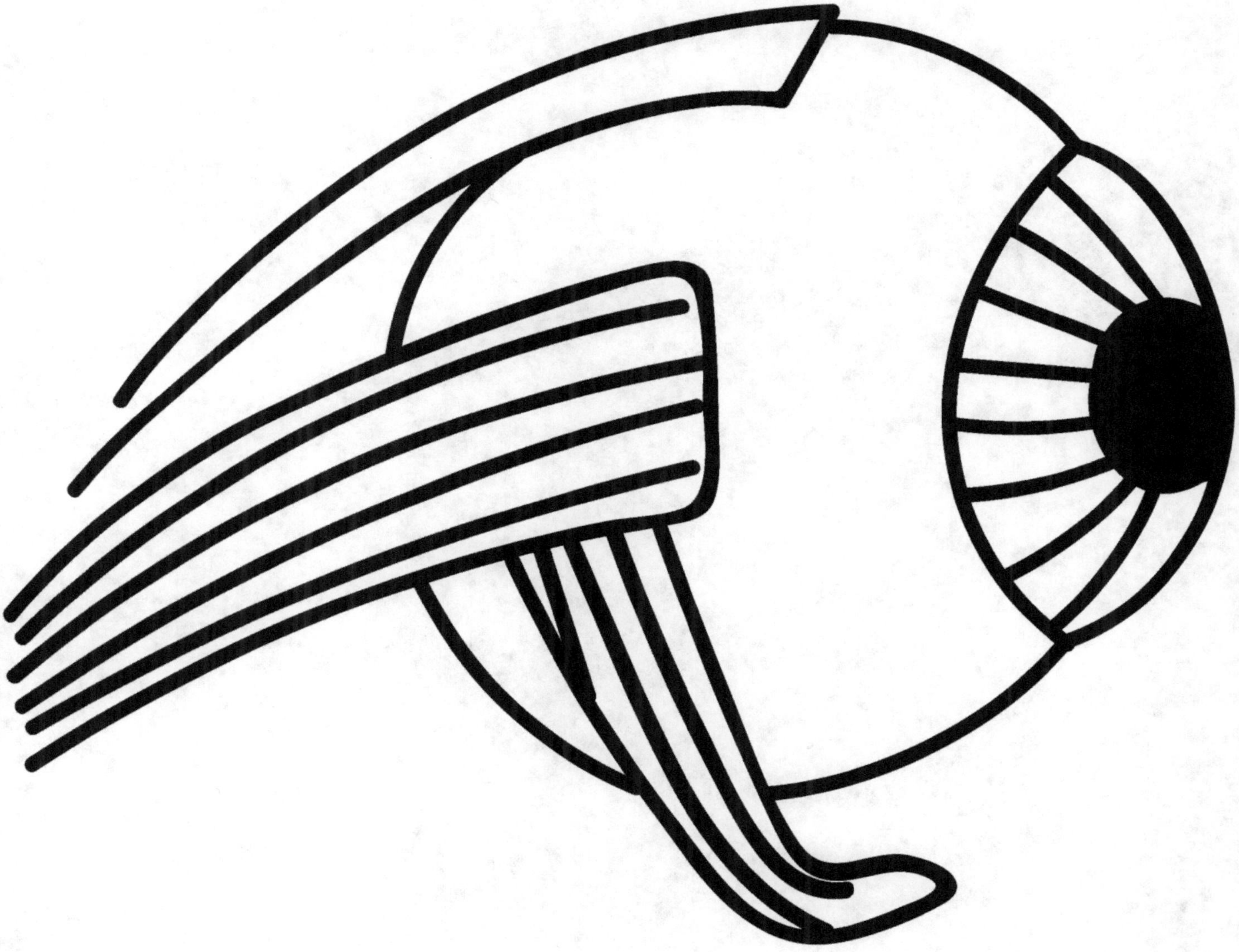

EYE BALL

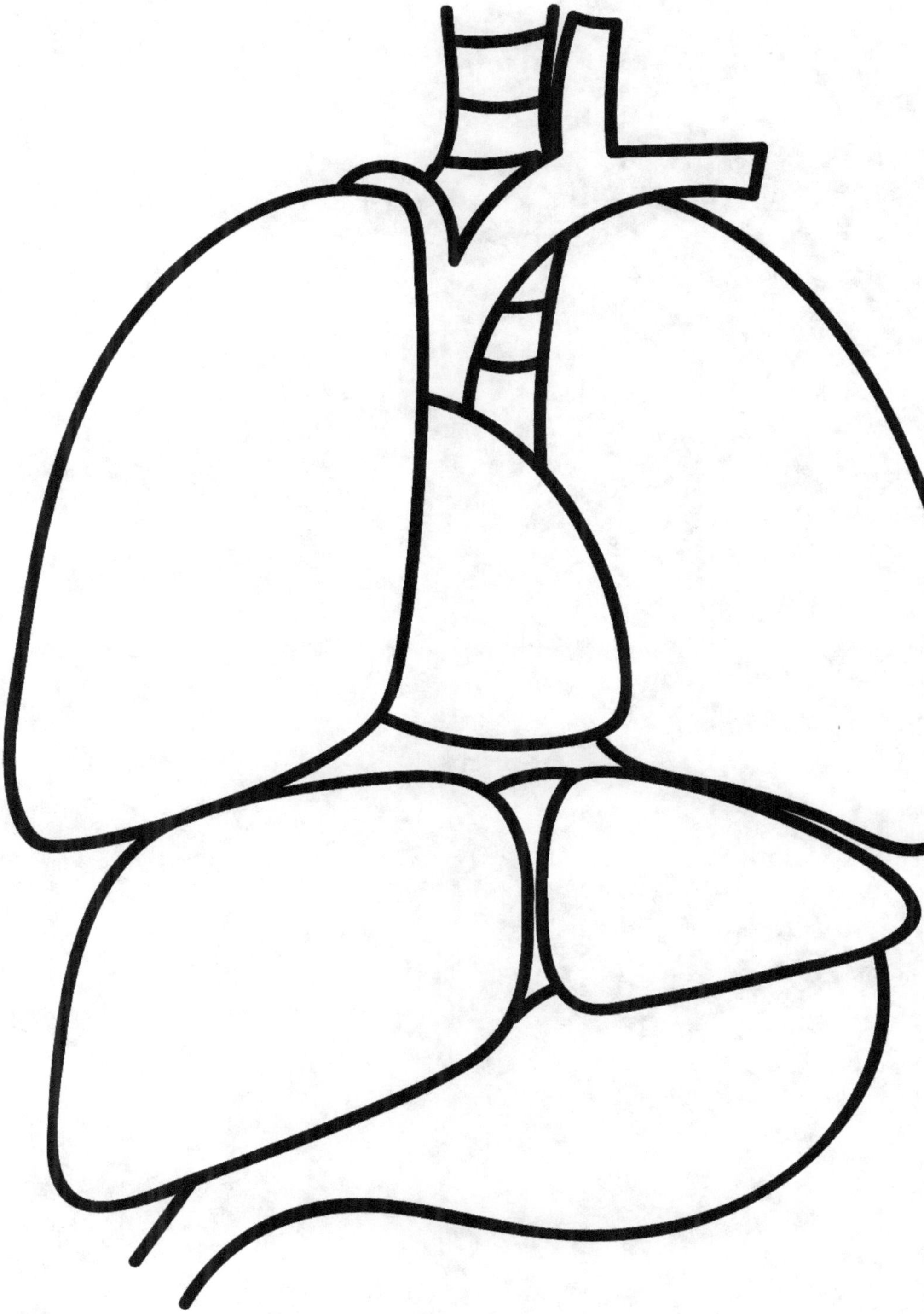

ORGANS

SKIN

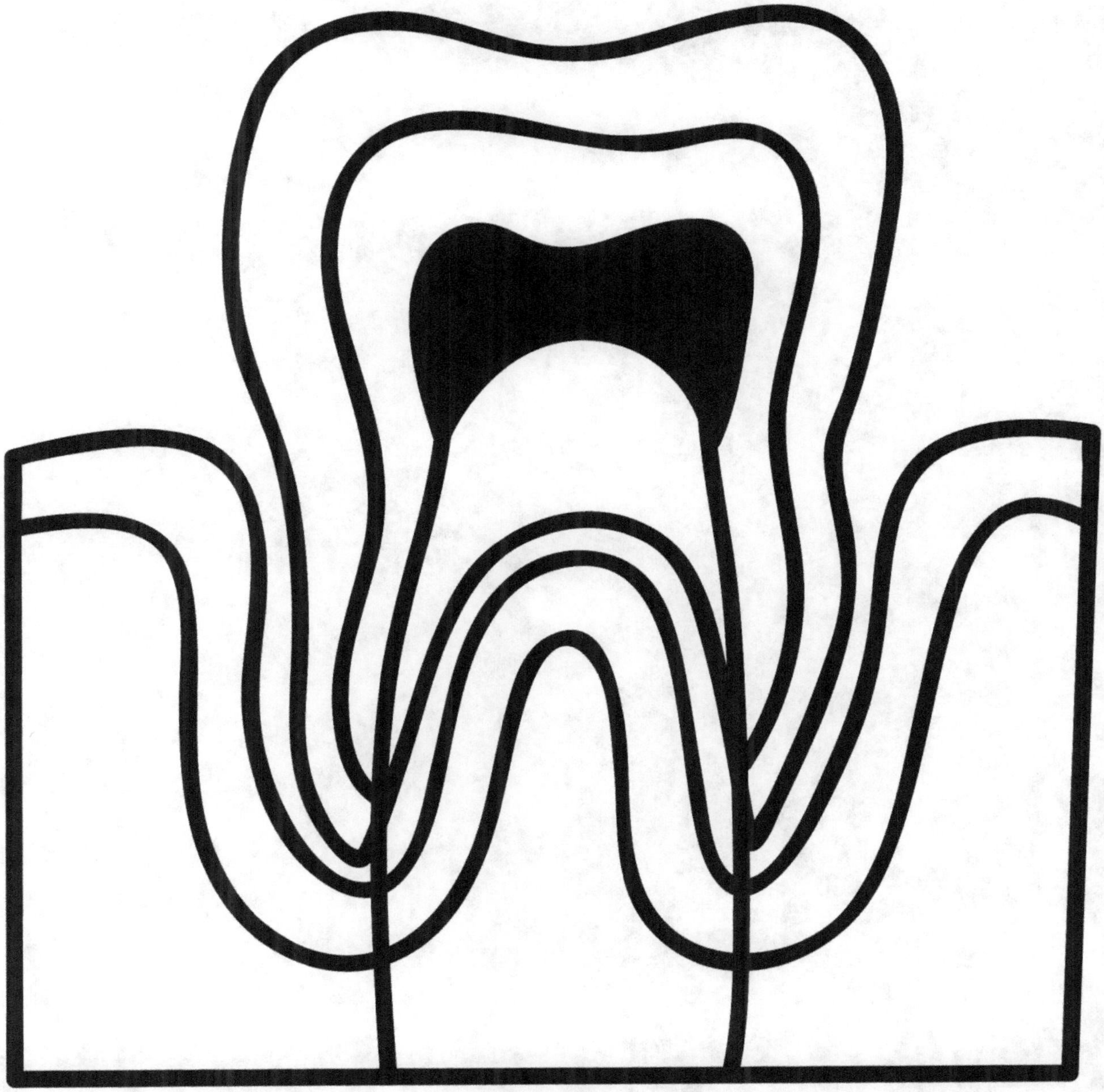

TOOTH

THYROID

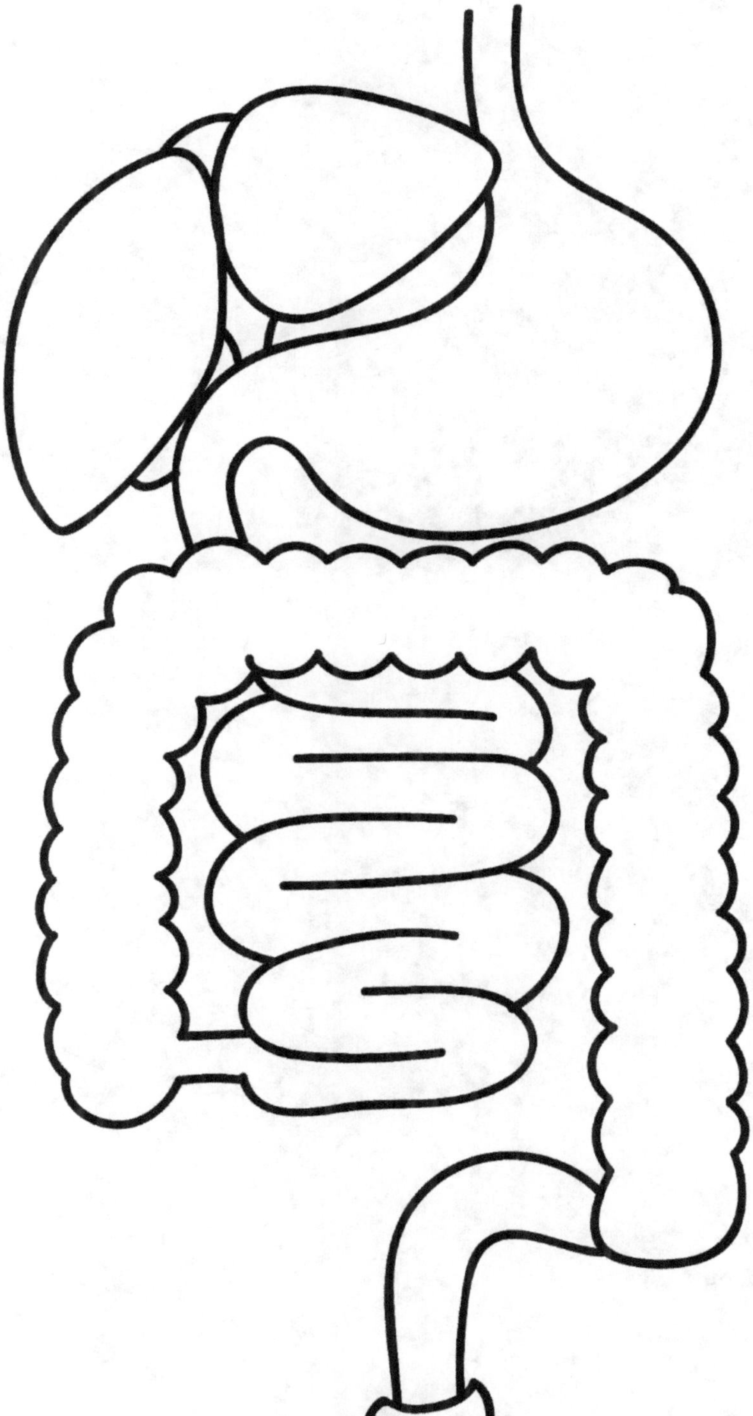

ORGANS

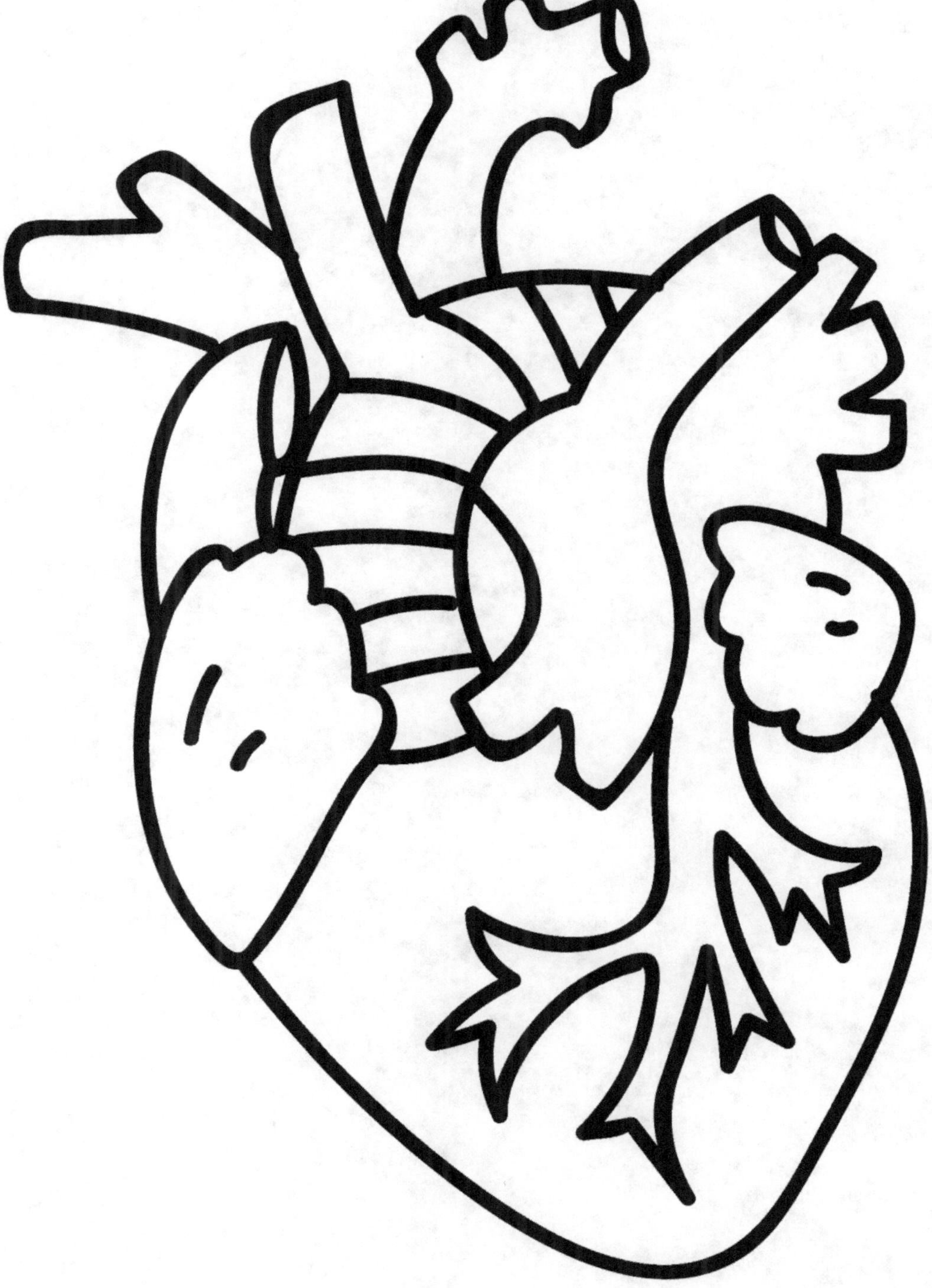

HEART

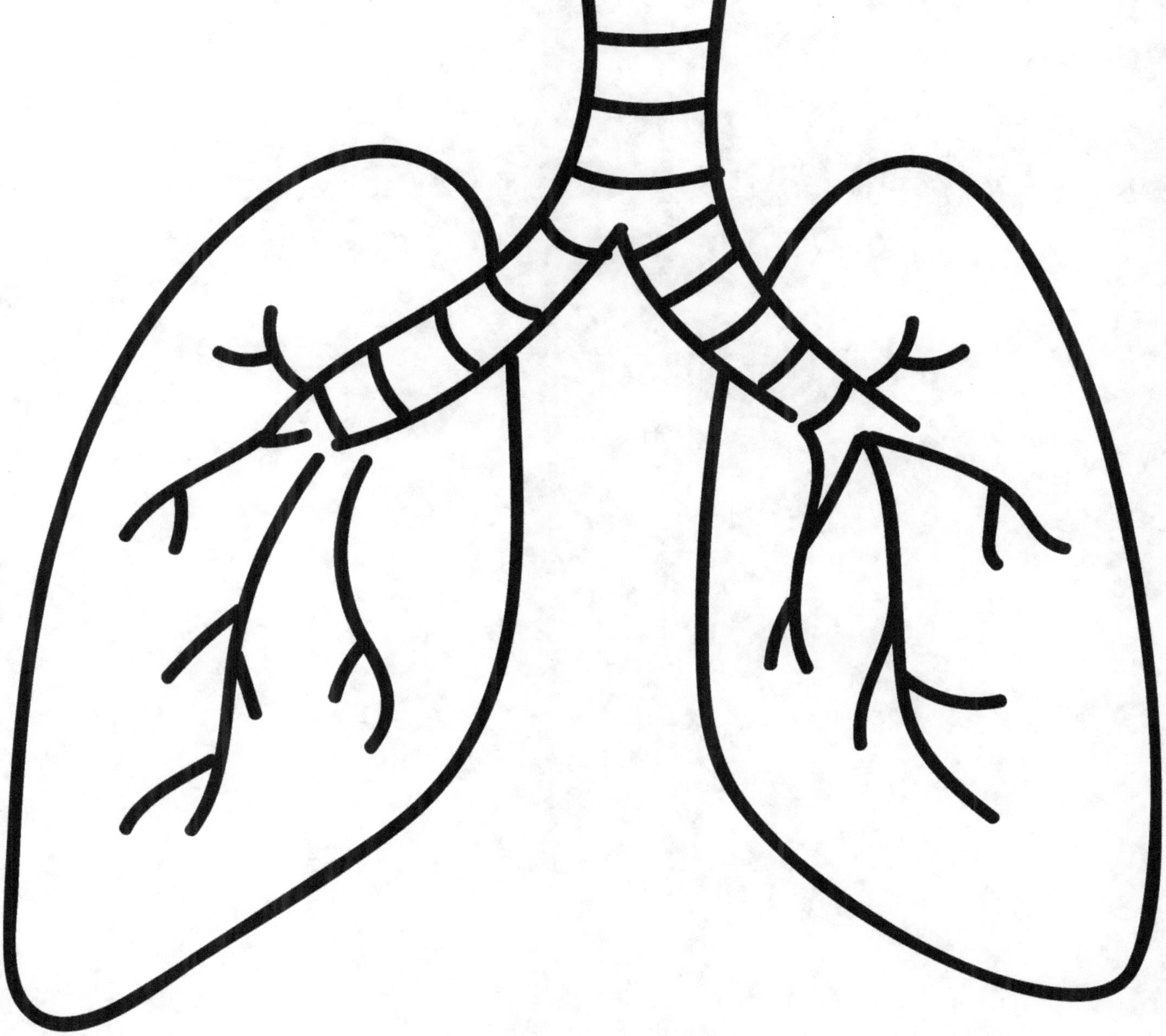

LUNG

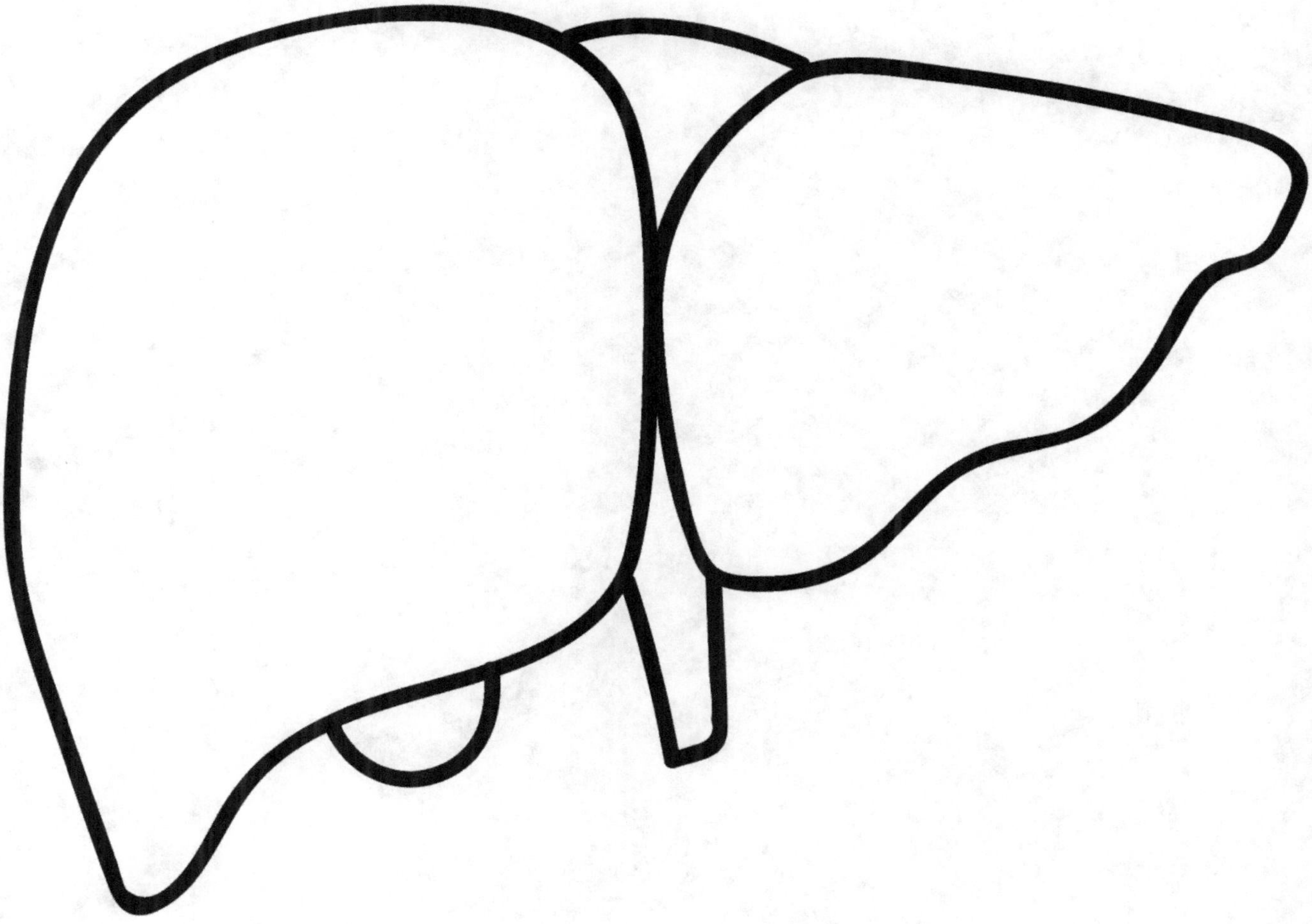

LIVER

SMALL INTESTINE

COLON

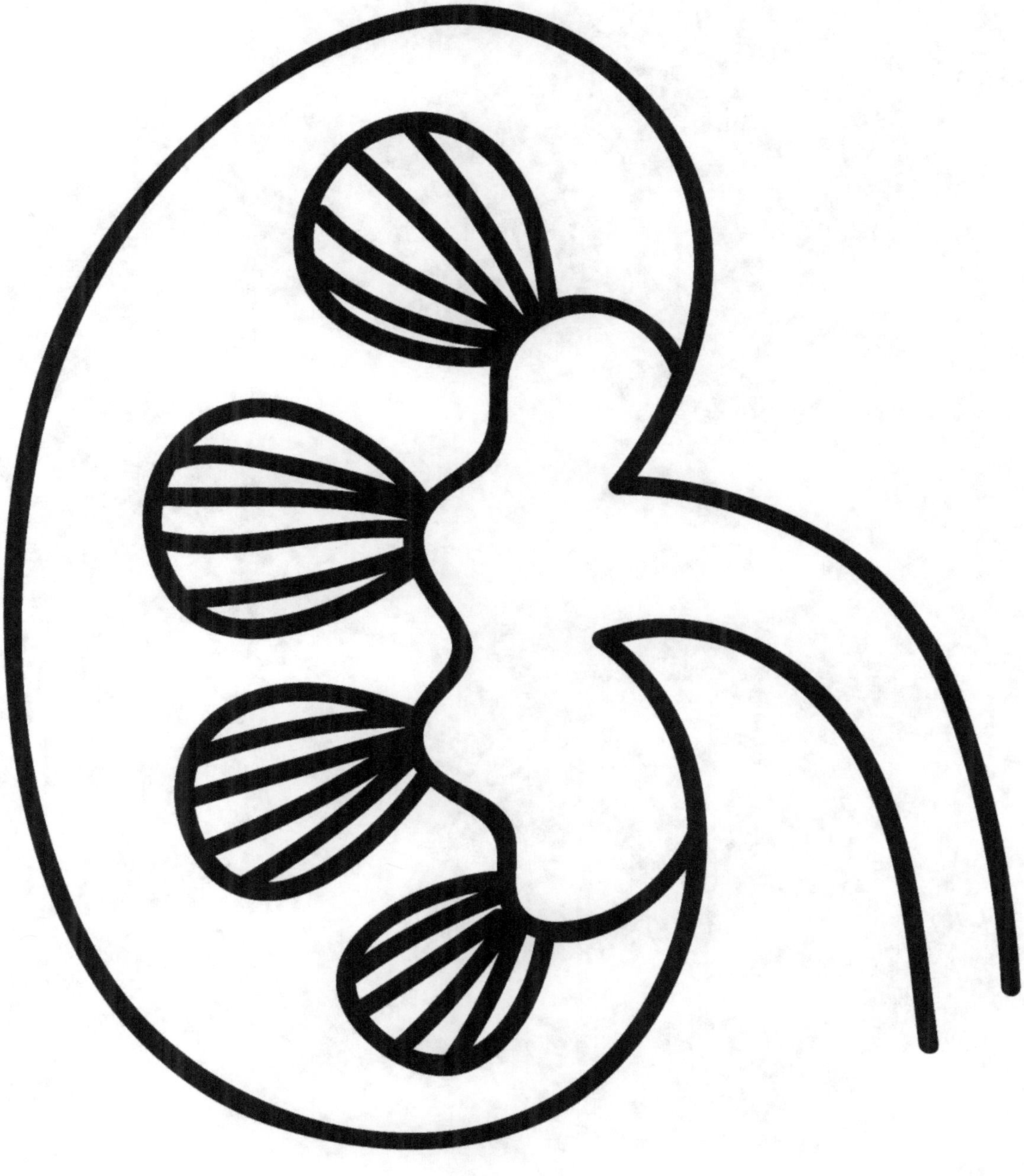

KIDNEY

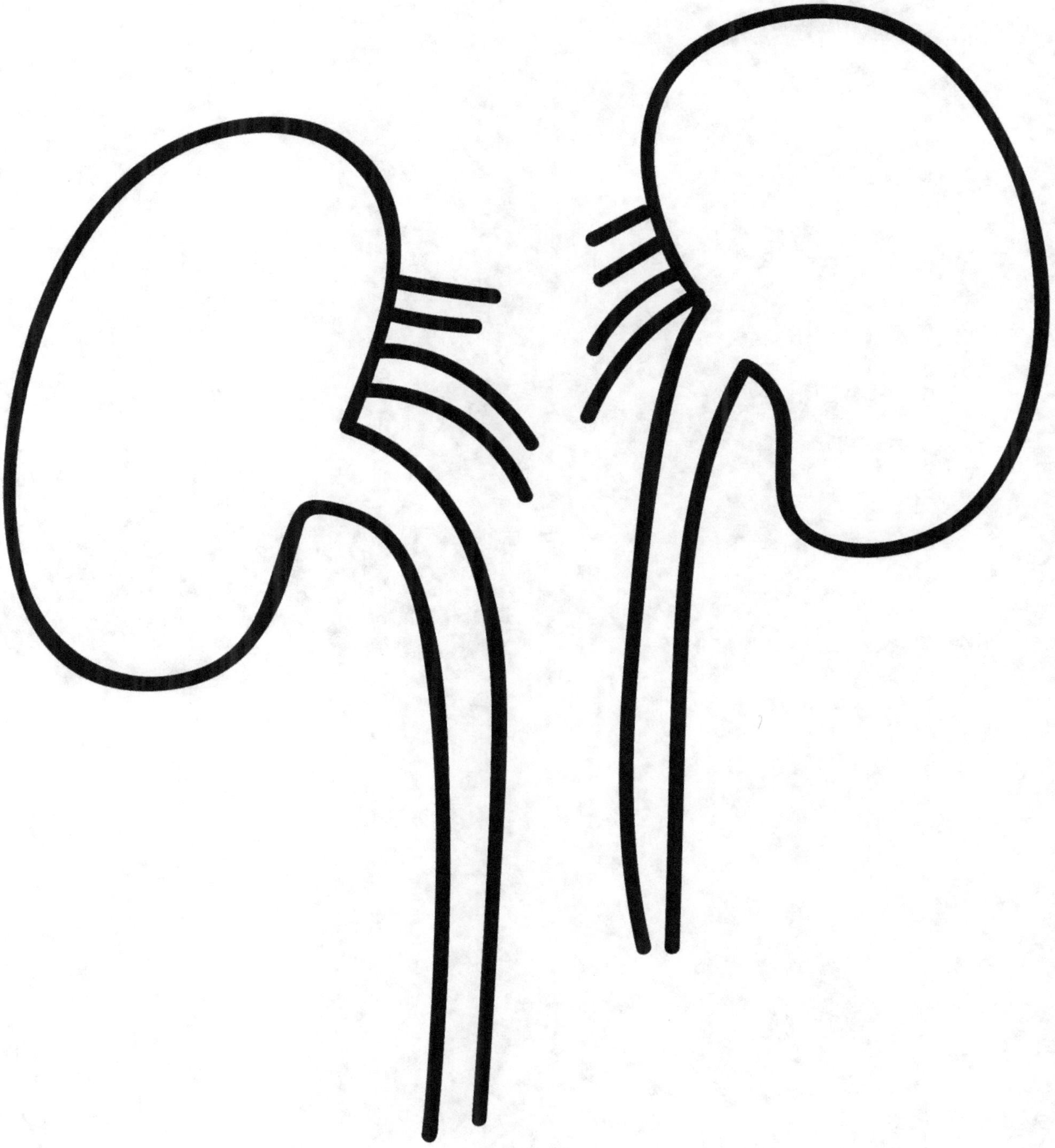

KIDNEYS

PANCREAS

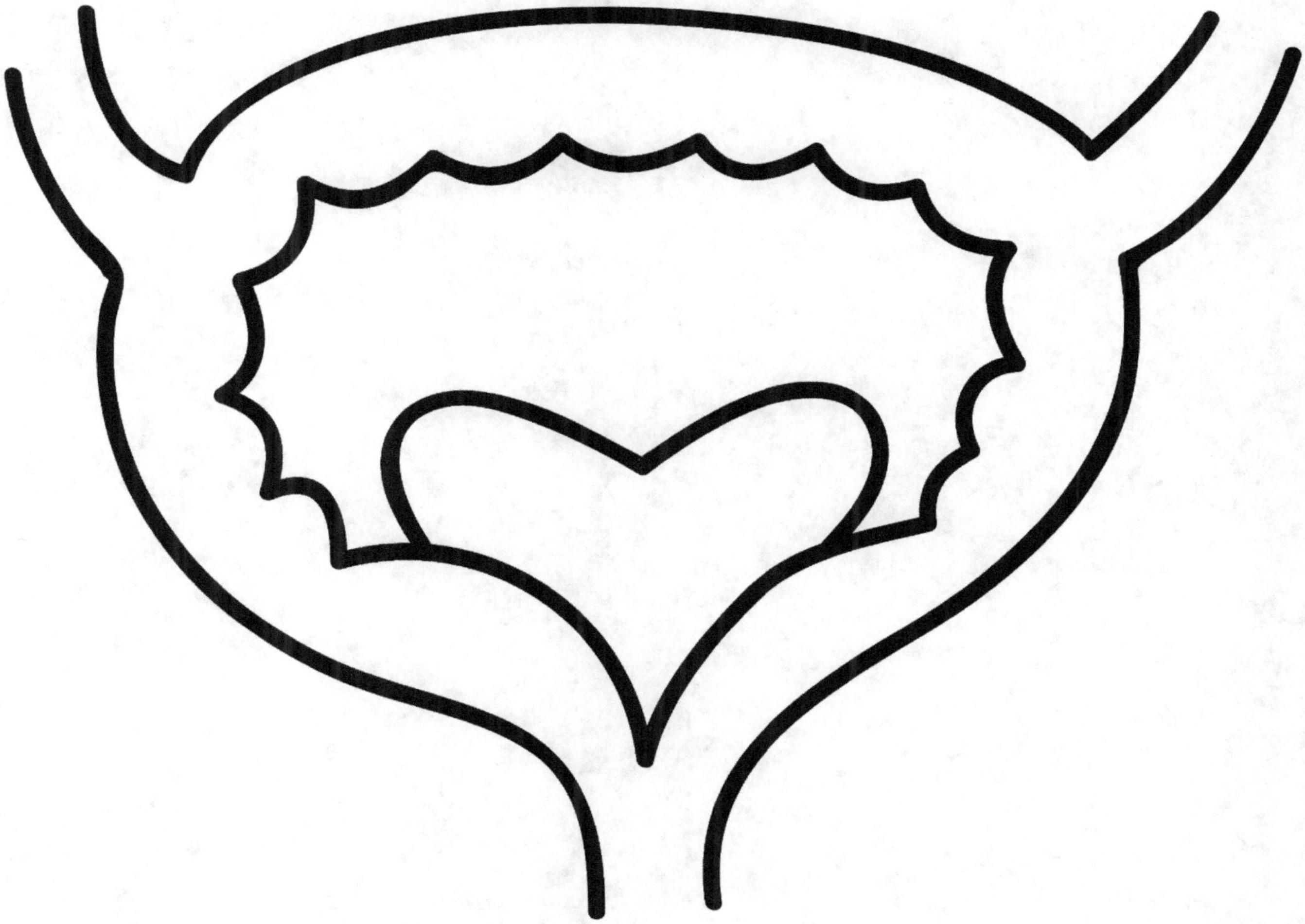

BLADDER

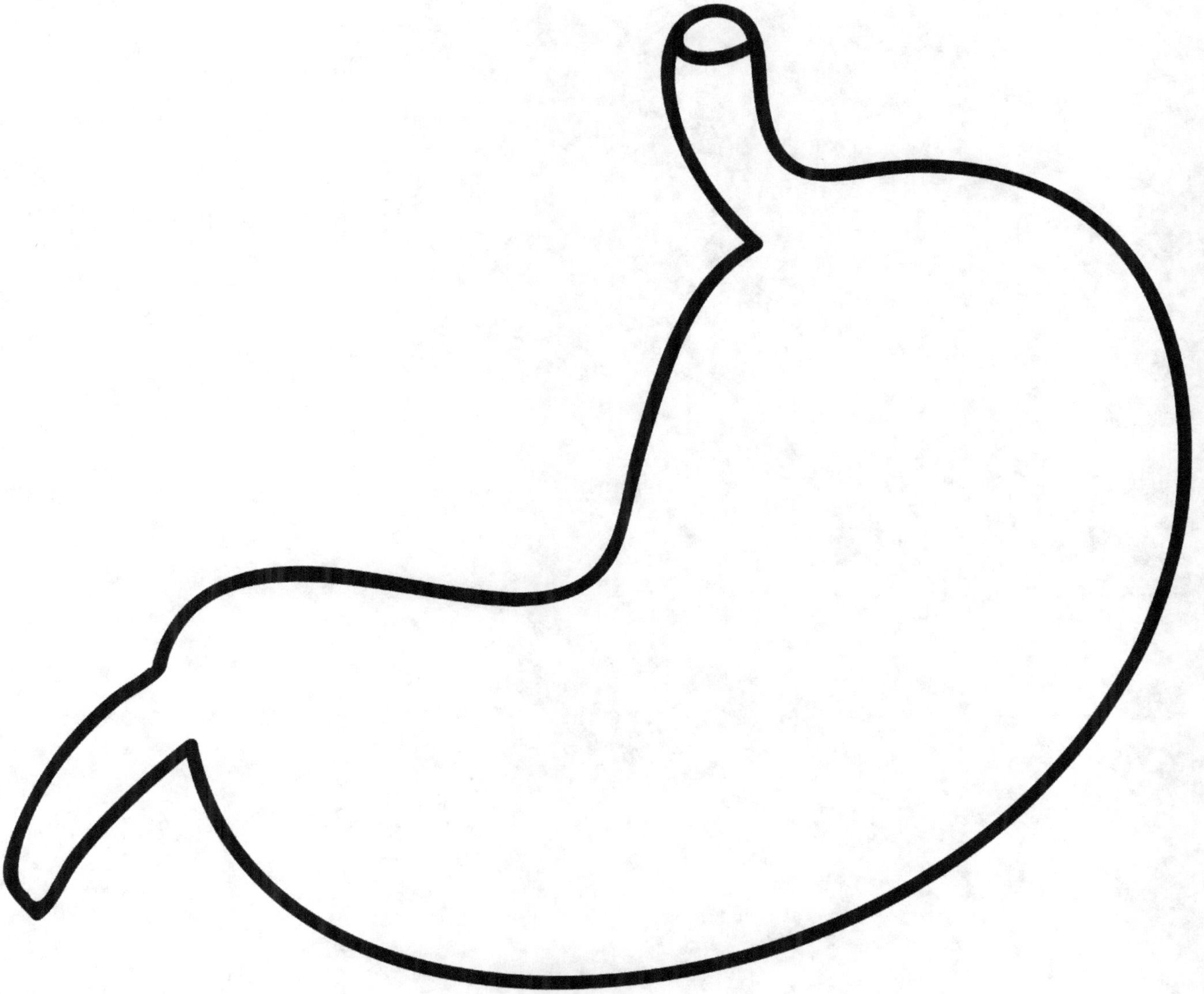

STOMACH

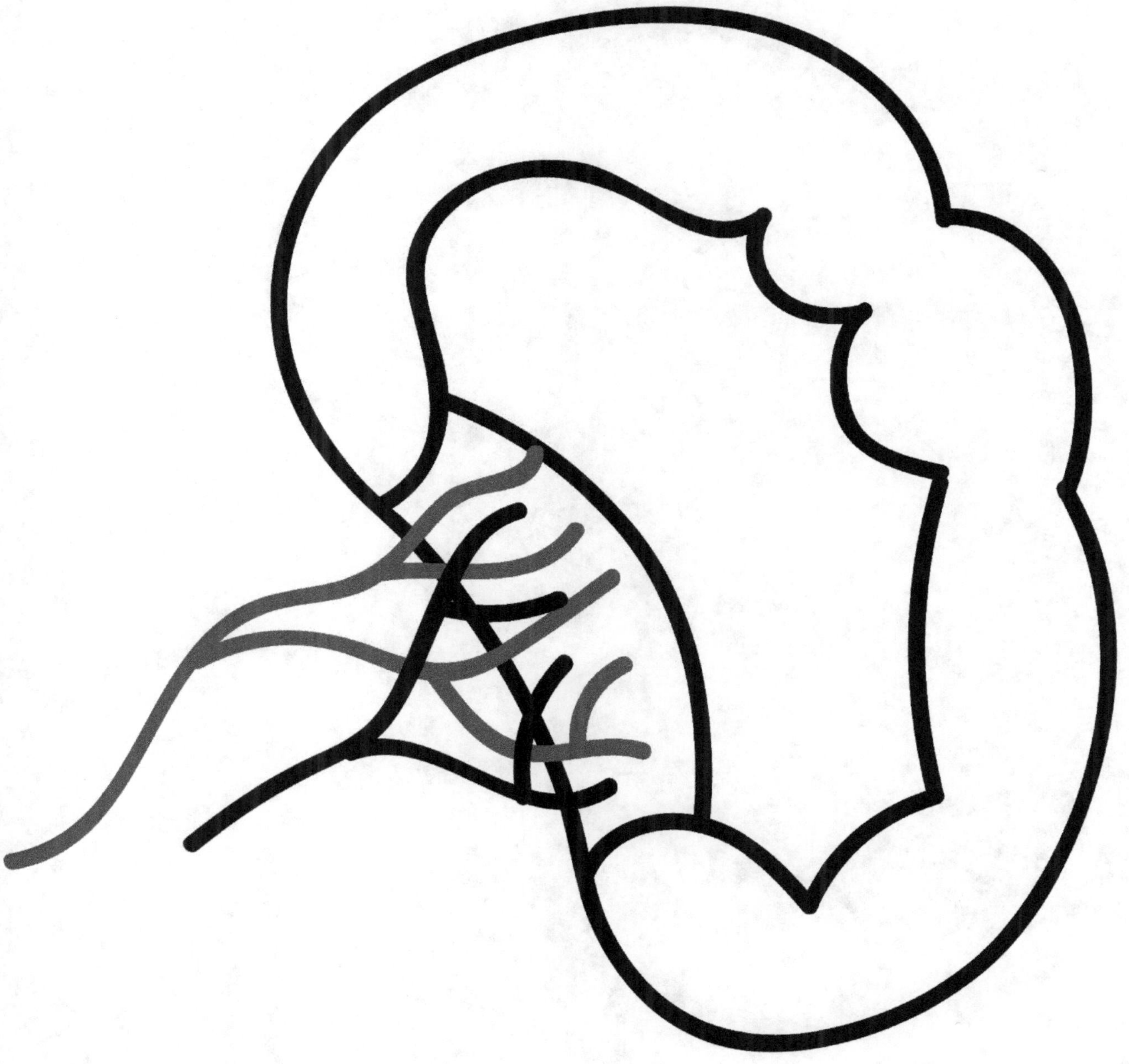

SPLEEN

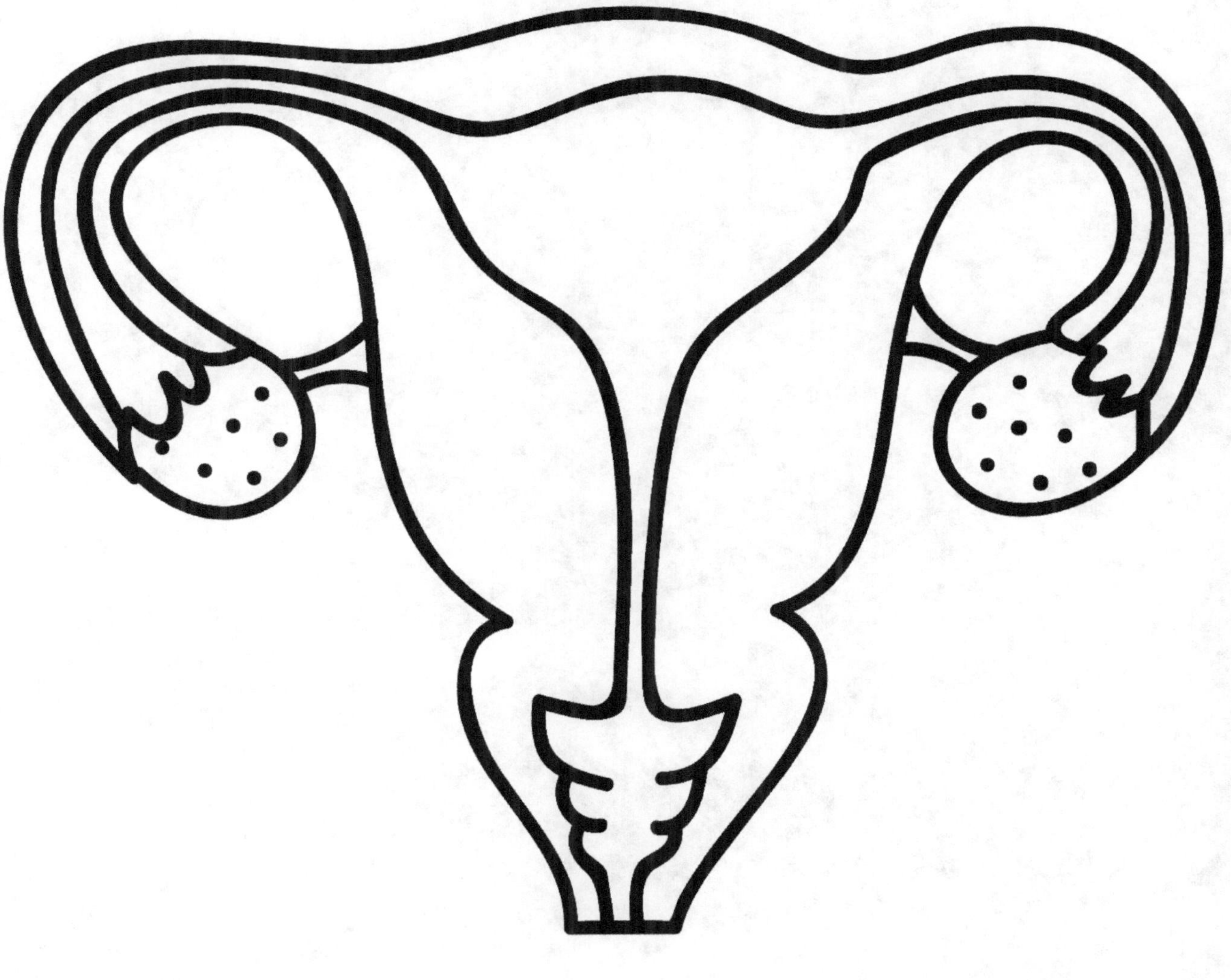

UTERUS

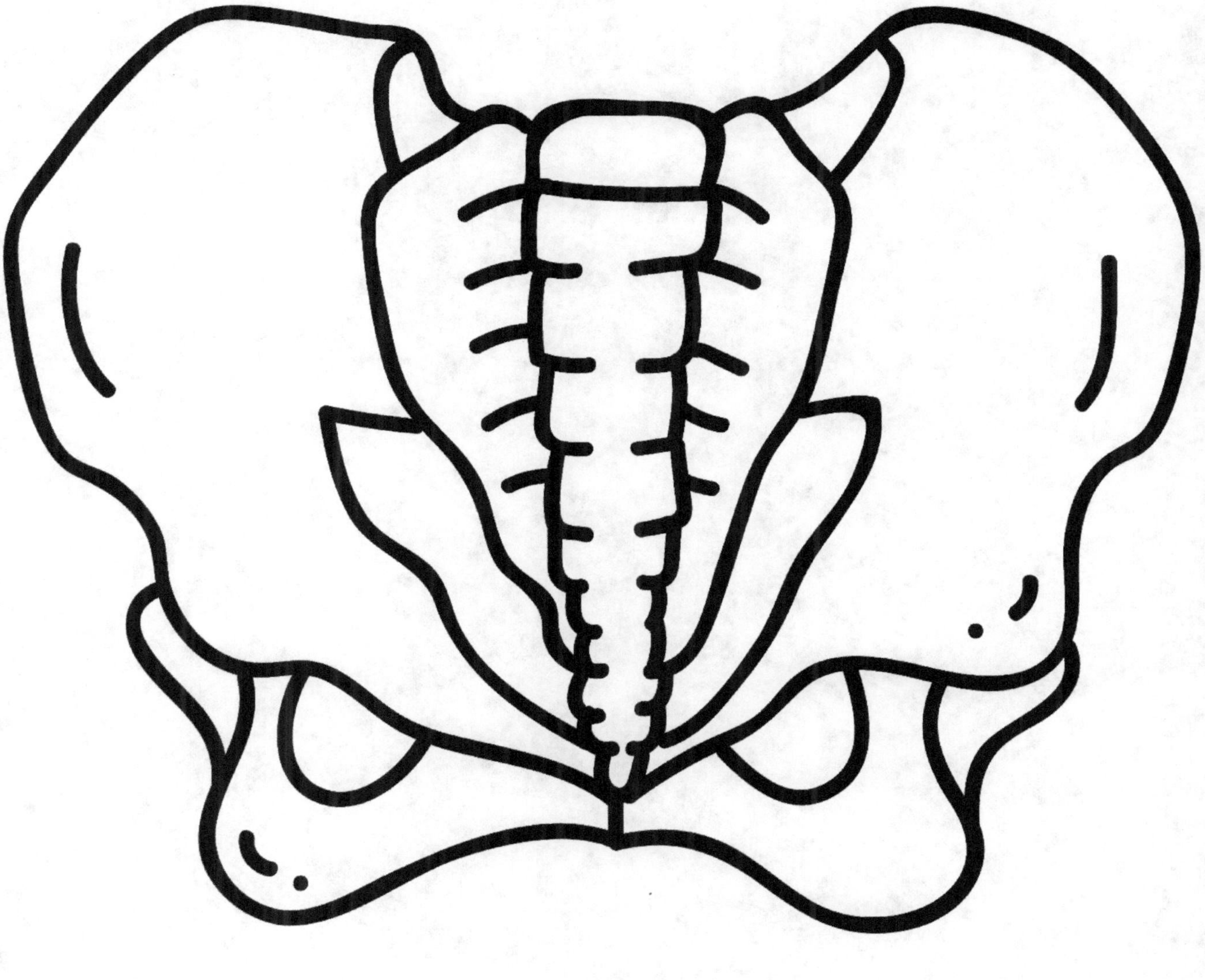

PELVIS

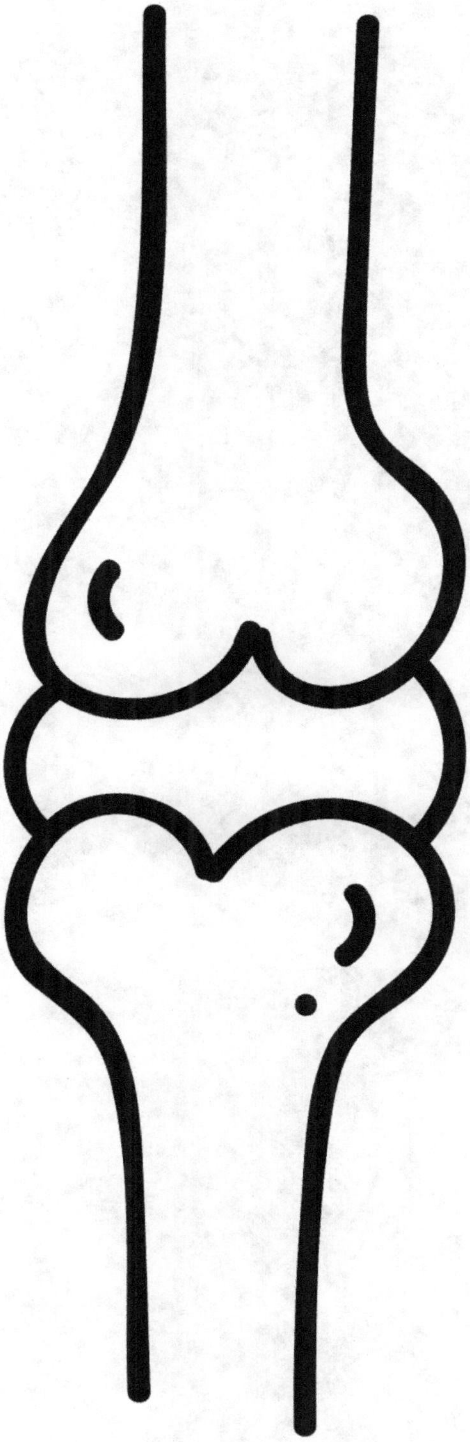

JOINT

EAR

NOSE

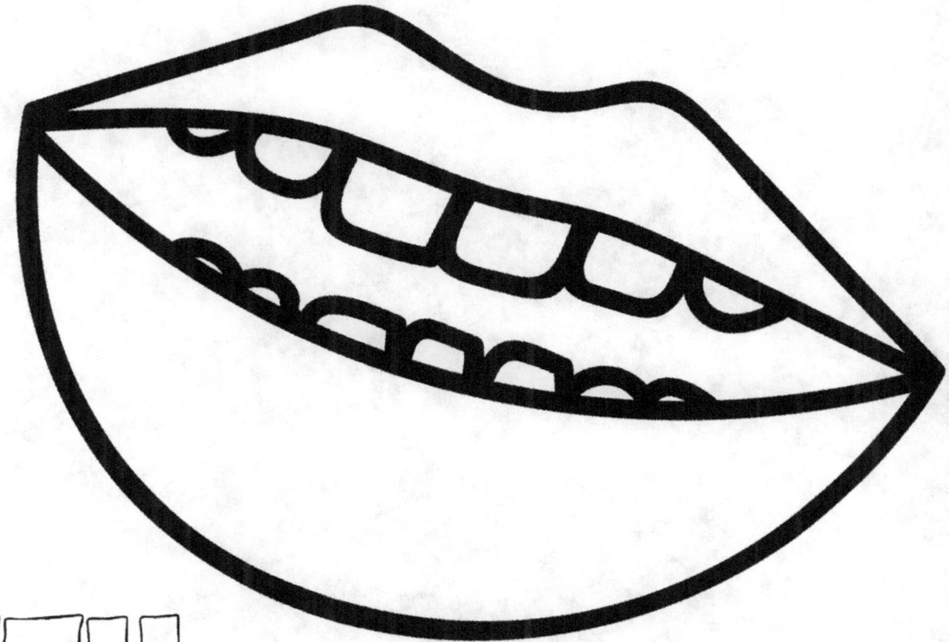

MOUTH

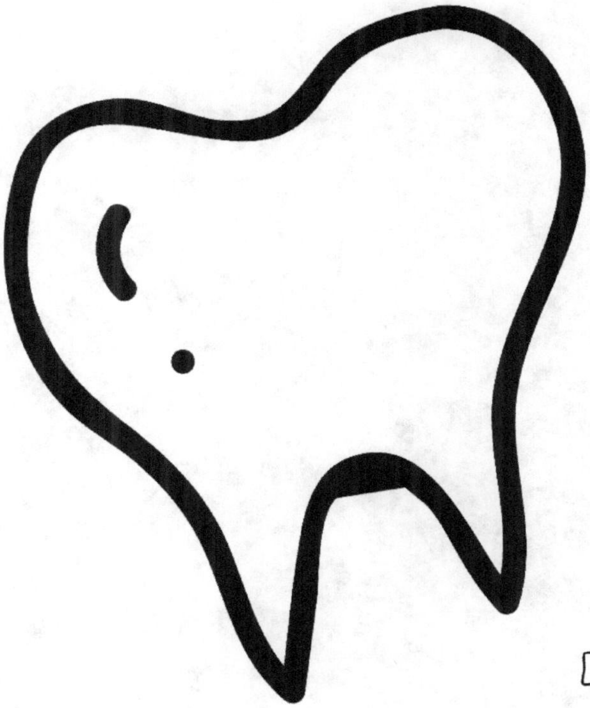

TOOTH

www.ingramcontent.com/pod-product-compliance
Lightning Source LLC
Chambersburg PA
CBHW081702220526
45466CB00009B/2853
* 9 7 9 8 5 8 2 0 9 3 2 3 7 *